Emeraldalicious

WRITTEN AND ILLUSTRATED
BY **Victoria Kann**

HARPER

An Imprint of HarperCollinsPublishers

Kann, Victoria.
Emeraldalicious / written and illustrated by Victoria Kann. — 1st ed.
        p.   cm.
Summary: Recycling magic turns a garbage-filled park into a "greenatastic" garden.
ISBN 978-0-06-225810-6 (international edition)
[1. Recycling (Waste)—Fiction.   2. Green movement—Fiction.   3. Magic—Fiction.]   I. Title.
PZ7.K12774Em   2013   2012009694   [E]—dc23   CIP   AC

The artist used mixed media to create the digital illustrations for this book.
Typography by Rachel Zegar   12 13 14 15 16   CG/WOR   10 9 8 7 6 5 4 3 2 1
❖
First Edition

For Maria M.

You!

I was strolling in the park with my brother, Peter.

Suddenly I tripped on a rock and fell, breaking my tiara and wand.

"Oh no! Look at your wand! You never go anywhere without it,"
said Peter. "What are you going to do?"

"I have an idea! I'll make a new one out of this stick," I said.

"And you can use these vines," said Peter.
"And that flower!" I said, pointing to a plant
I had never seen before.

"I love you, pretty wand!" I said, kissing the wand.

The wand began to sparkle.

"Wow! Did you see that?" said Peter.

"Are you a MAGIC wand?" I asked, and the wand flew out of my hand.

"Come back here!" I yelled. The wand did not listen to me.

"I am Pinkalicious, the Princess of Pink, and I command you to return to me!"

The wand paused, and then flew farther up the path.

"Maybe it isn't listening to you because you don't have a crown or a cape like a real princess," said Peter.

"You're right!" I said. I picked some flowers and made a crown. Then I tied leaves together and wove flowers to make a cape.

"I am the Princess of Flowers!" I announced.

When we turned the corner, I found the magic wand on a pile of garbage.

"Yuck!" said Peter. "It smells."

I reached for the wand, but it flew up into a tree.

"What a sad tree! Its leaves are dropping." I climbed the tree and grabbed my magic wand.

"This is where we had picnics! What happened?" asked Peter.

"This used to be my favorite park," I said.

Suddenly there was a loud crack. The tree swayed,
and the branch that I was sitting on broke.
I fell to the ground with a thud.
"OUCH!"

"Harrumph! I need a chair."
I waved the magic wand and said,

"Buckets, bow tie and a bone.
All this garbage makes me groan.
What I would love is a pretty throne."

Garbage started flying through the sky and then magically
transformed into a throne.

"Did that REALLY happen?" I gasped.
"Wow! You should make a castle!" said Peter.
"Make a castle!" I commanded.
Nothing happened.

"What a silly wand!" I said, and threw it to the ground.

The wand sparkled.

"It has to work, since it worked before and made the throne!" insisted Peter.

"Hmm, what did I say when I made the throne?" I asked Peter.

Peter giggled, imitating me in a high-pitched voice—
"You said, 'What I would love . . .'"
"Look, Peter! When you said 'love', a little flower bloomed!
Love," I whispered. Another flower opened.
"Love," I said again, and a third flower blossomed.

"Suitcase, snorkel, stinky shoe.
I love pink, purple and blue.
Make me flowers in every hue!"

I waved my magic wand, and flowers grew out of the ground.

"HEY, HOW DID YOU DO THAT?" asked Peter.
"It's easy! Take the wand, describe what is around
you and ask for what you want with love . . ."
"And make up a rhyme!" added Peter.
"Watch me," I said.

"Grapefruit, girdle and a glove.
Make a place filled with love.
Bring in birds from up above!"

Garbage started flying in a million directions, and colourful, twittering birds appeared.

"Let me try!" Peter begged, and quickly said,

"Television, towel and a tassel.
I'm a prince who loves his castle.
Please make me one without a hassle!"

A castle appeared.
"IT WORKS! Look, it even has a moat! It took the
garbage and made a castle! I can't believe it!" said Peter.
"Wow! What else can we make?"

"I know . . ." I said.

"Telephone, teacup and twine.
I'd love a dress that's really fine.
Take this trash and make it mine!"

Right before my eyes, a beautiful new outfit was made.

"Now I'll make something for you, Peter.

"Hairbrush, hanger, harp and heel.
What I love is this old wheel..." I said.

"Recycle it into a boat mobile!" finished Peter.

"Let me do it. This is fun!" Peter said, grabbing the wand.
"I want to make a cookie-candy-cupcake-ice-cream machine that
makes a different flavour of sweets every ten minutes, and a robot
to clean my room, and then a great big rocket!"

"Peter, come back here NOW! I'll share with you, but it's MY turn,
and I have a really good wish!"

"Let's fix this garbage dump," I said. "It sure is ugly and stinky!

"Detergent, doughnut and dirty dishes.
Pinkalicious loves her wishes.
Make this place Emeraldalicious!"

I waved my magic wand . . .
. . . and the dump transformed
into a greenatastic garden.

Just then, there was a gust of wind. The magic wand broke apart and filled the sky with sparkly seeds.

"OH NO! What are we going to do without the
wand? We can't make things happen anymore."
Peter cried, "The magic is gone!"

"Don't worry, Peter. We still have everything we need!" I said. "We have these seeds, and with a little love we can make the entire world EMERALDALICIOUS!"

"And that would be greenerrific!" said Peter.

Made in the USA
San Bernardino, CA
16 December 2017

CAN YOU GUESS THEIR NAMES?

WHAT FUN WE HAD LEARNING
TO TREAT ALL LIFE
WITH RESPECT AND CARE.

HAMSTER

"HAMSTERS LIKE TO HAVE
THEIR BACKS
GENTLY RUBBED."

"PONIES LIKE TO HAVE THEIR SNOUTS RUBBED."

BIRD

BUNNY

"BUNNIES LIKE TO
HAVE THEIR BACKS
RUBBED."

DOG

"DOGS LIKE TO HAVE THEIR TUMMIES SCRATCHED."

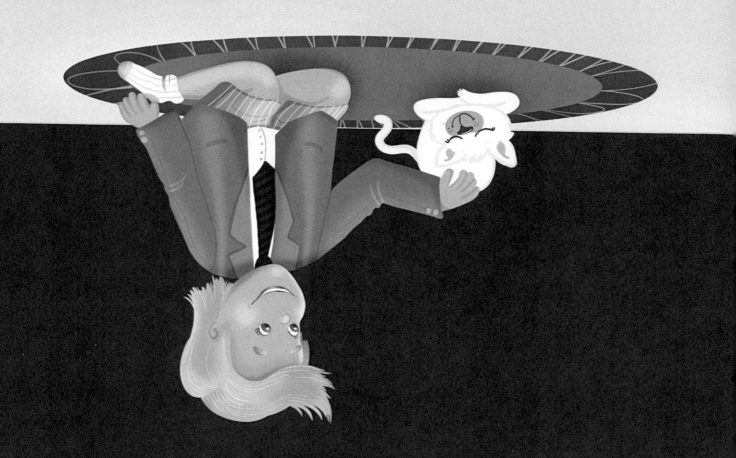

PUSSY CAT

"PUSSY CATS LIKE TO
HAVE THEIR
BACKS RUBBED."

Dedication

To Carrie: I will always get permission first. Love you

To Teagan: May you continue to make reading your daily practice. Love you.

To Barbara: Thank you for everything. Love you

To Kathie: Sorry I drooled on your arm. Love you

Donald Don't Grab that Pussy

Written by Mike McAffen

Illustrated by Lovyaa Garg